The Unleashed Entrepreneur

A Kick-Ass Guide To
Harnessing Your Inner Ninja,
Working Less,
& Creating Your Perfect Lifestyle

Mitche Graf

The Unleashed Entrepreneur: A Kick-Ass Guide to Harnessing Your Inner Ninja, Working Less, & Creating Your Perfect Lifestyle.

© 2018 Mitche Graf.

Editing: Free Eagle Studios, LLC
Cover Design: David Thompson
Back Cover Photo: Tami Graf

Publisher: Power Marketing 101
P.O. Box 405
Aurora, Oregon 97002
USA

FOR BULK ORDERS OR GROUP DISCOUNTS CALL:
888.719.4692

www.PowerMarketing101.com

ISBN: 978-1-7320344-1-9

Table of Contents

About Your Captain For This Flight

Daddy, author, serial entrepreneur, international-renowned business speaker, and amateur gardener Mitche Graf has been a passionate entrepreneur for over 25 years, dangling his toes into the ponds of many intriguing industries along the way. From selling used bicycle parts out of his garage in the seventh grade to running three companies today, he has prided himself on knowing how to squeeze every drop of potential out of his endeavors.

Over the past three decades, Mitche has created two award-winning restaurants, a bustling catering & events company, a national spice manufacturing business with over 4000 accounts, a photography studio, a cribbage board company, an award-winning limousine business, a portable hot tub rental business, a drive-through espresso company, an educational products company, an athletic fitness testing corporation, and even a night crawler company.

Having started, built, and successfully operated numerous enterprises in a multitude of industries has taught him a simple truth: the same basic business principles apply, regardless of the arena you may play in.

As an educator and motivational speaker, Mitche's high-voltage seminars and workshops have been delivered around the world to over 75,000 people in nine countries and nearly every state in the U.S. His cutting-edge articles and columns have appeared in the pages of business trade magazines such as *Rangefinder*, *PPA Magazine*, *Limo Digest*, *Chauffer Driven*, *Image Maker*, and *Fresh Cup*, as well as many online marketing sites and blogs.

A majority of his education and training has been from the School of Hard Knocks, from which he has earned his Master's degree. Through the high-notes of his business home runs, to the low-notes of bankruptcy in the 1990s, Mitche has continued to make bold attempts to redefine the limits of his abilities, and to reinvent the way his businesses operate so they don't become all-consuming black holes that suck him dry of his creative juices and zest for life.

Getting punched in the face from failure is probably the best teacher he has ever had and most of the lessons he has learned were born out of those failures.

He firmly believes life is meant to be lived, not endured, and we each can make a profound difference in the world. He loves his family, loves his friends, and the rest just falls into place!

He is passionate about the outdoors, and laughing, playing guitar, reading, listening to great music, cooking and eating, drinking good wine, taking a tremendous amount of time off to chill, and most importantly, spending time with his family.

Mitche lives in a small country town in Oregon with his wife Tami and their three small children Jaycee, Colton, and Sierra, Tilly the Dog, Nickels the Bunny, Coral the Hermit Crab, and several hundred guppies (names not important).

He spends much of his time looking for ways to work smarter, not harder, so he can spend more time doing and enjoying the things in life that are most important to him.

He believes that EVERY DAY IS A SATURDAY, and this perspective inspires him to wake up every day with a sense of excitement and enthusiasm to live his life by design.

Sit back, relax, and enjoy the flight.

The journey you are about to take can potentially change your life forever. Buckle up and let's get rockin'!

Chapter 1
The Awakening

I haven't worked a single day since the spring of 1994.

That was the day I left my job as National Sales Manager & Vice-President of Marketing for a large pet product manufacturing company. Instead, I decided to become a full-time entrepreneur. I can hear you whistle, "Man, what a stupid move."

Especially since it was a great job with extraordinary pay. I drove a nice sports car and had an active social life, but I wasn't completely happy. I wasn't hitting on all cylinders. Something was lacking from my spirit. There was a void, and I needed to find out what was missing. I needed to unleash my entrepreneurial DNA and see what new adventures and undiscovered lands I could conquer with my ideas.

I felt overworked, under-appreciated, trapped in a 9-5 executive office, and addicted to being a workaholic. My days started early and ended late. Reviewing budgets, creating sales pitches, sales projections, screening resumes, and meeting with ownership.

All these time-sucking activities meant my brain didn't have a chance to recharge or re-energize, and inevitably, the lines between my personal life and my stressful job became blurred beyond recognition. I made the decision to make the jump, then I just jumped!

I knew I was in for challenges that I never had to deal with before. No more *atta-boys* from superiors or bonus checks for jobs well done. I was about to unleash my spirit from the self-imposed prison I'd built around my passion for so many years.

I was determined to become one of the chosen few to blaze a new business trail and retake control of my life.

By far, the most valuable asset that you and I possess is time, and the biggest decision we have on a daily basis is how we choose to spend it. We have 86,400 seconds each day. How we consciously choose to spend those seconds determines who we ultimately become over our lifetime.

Each day, we literally make hundreds of decisions determining what kind of successes or failures our businesses will have to endure. Many of these seconds, minutes, and hours are wasted on thoughts and activities that add zero value to our lives or the lives of the people who mean the most to us.

And once that time is spent, we can never get it back.

Leaving my corporate job provided a real shock to my system. The School of Hard Knocks was about to open its' doors to me. A If I didn't' do it correctly, there would be a deep grave of failed business corpses was waiting at the end of the proverbial hallway of doom.

I knew my chances for success were low. I was aware half of all businesses ended within the first year, 80% gone within five years, and 96% failed within 10 years. I had started and built several businesses before then, but this was the first time I was going to be "all-in" with no fallback position. For those of you who have started a business at some point in your life, you know exactly what I'm talking about.

Even with doom and gloom staring at me in the face, my only thought was: *Hooray, I'm going to be one of the 4% who will make it as an entrepreneur!*

There's an excitement that wells up inside, a surreal calm that overtakes the inner fears of the prospective businessperson. In fact, the excitement can be so magnificent that it's difficult to shut down the river of creative ideas flowing at every waking moment of the day.

I knew my odds were low, but I had a big advantage over failure. I had the rare ability to treat EVERY DAY LIKE IT

WAS A SATURDAY! I don't get the Monday morning blues or get stuck in the rut of a 9-5 mentality work week.

This life-changing philosophy was instilled in me by my stepfather, Pat Wright, one of the hardest working men I've ever met. He loved my Mom deeply, and that motivated him to do whatever was necessary to keep us safe and secure.

My parents divorced when I was eleven, and my Mom worked 2-3 jobs to provide for my brother, sister, and me. We would see Dad on weekends, but the day-to-day raising of us kids was all Mom. Pat came into our lives several years later, and by that time we were a tribe of hardened souls accustomed to doing without in many cases, but never lacking in the important things in life.

When I was in my early 20s, Mom and Pat dreamed of owning a boat. Not a big, fancy boat to sail the seven seas in, just a boat the family could take to Hayden Lake in North Idaho to spend our weekends floating off into warm, summer evenings.

With this dream in mind, they managed to set aside enough money to realize their dream. They eventually found and bought *Big Red,* an old V-hulled Fiberform. The excitement in our family was incredibly palpable. She was an older vessel that needed a paint job and some TLC, but she had class.

We bought Pat his very first captain's hat, loaded the cooler with beer, and set sail.

I distinctly remember to this day how the five of us left the marina with smiles-in-tow on a beautiful summer day. With our troubles behind us, we fell into total silence as we looked around and oohed at the beautiful mountains and shorelines.

We were without a care in the world, at least at that moment. Nobody was going to take away the beauty of that moment from us.

The awesome silence was broken by Pat's immortal words.

"I wonder what the poor folk are doing today?"

Those words hit home. We suddenly felt elevated to a higher plane at that singular moment. We were all in Never-Never land for that tiny little slice of our awesome day that nobody could take away from us. An amazing feeling of euphoria floated in our minds, however fleetingly.

My mother responded, "Babe, we are the poor folk."

Her words were true to the core in the practical sense, but on that day, practicality was out the window.

Pat affectionately looked at each of us, then looked out over the horizon with his chest puffed up, head held high, and said:

"Not today babe, not today."

At that precise moment, we became the richest people on Planet Earth—and it had nothing to do with money!

It was about living in the moment, enjoying the gift of the present. It didn't matter what the following Monday was going to have in store for us, it was all about living like royalty at that very moment.

Pat was a superhero to me and my siblings. Every superhero has a power that emanates from within, that empowers them with a competitive edge and drive against negative and evil forces of the universe.

Thanks to Pat, one of my super powers is the ability to approach every single day like it's a Saturday!

Several years later, Pat was working as a parts manager for a Toyota dealership and loving his life with Mom. The kids were out of the house, and they were both living large.

One Monday afternoon, he grabbed his keys, had a quick laugh with his co-workers, and headed home to spend another cozy evening with his wife. But before he had the chance to open his office door, Pat collapsed.

He never made it home for dinner.

Happiness and optimism were in Pat's bones. Maybe it was from his days in Vietnam watching buddies die right in front of him, or maybe it was simply knowing something that the rest of us didn't. His unique way of looking at a miserable situation and making it bearable, in turning lemons into lemonade, making every day a Saturday, was his precious gift to me.

We spent the week talking about the good times, remembering the laughter, and crying until we didn't have any more tears left. As the week went along, our emotions seemed to elevate to the point that we laughed louder and cried bigger. When it was time for us to return to our lives, I can remember feeling like my entire spirit had just been cleansed. Amazingly, I felt like I had been gifted with a renewed sense of perspective for my own life.

I wouldn't trade that time for anything in the world. It's these moments in life that you talk about things you normally don't talk about. It made me realize that everyday can be a perfect "10" for my family, friends, co-workers, employees, and myself. I should never let a day go by that I don't tell the people who mean the most to me that I love them. Life is much too short to not do it!

Realize that every day can be a perfect 10-Day for you as well. The past is history, the future is unknowable. All you have is right now. That's it. You never know what lies around the corner. Of all the gifts I've received, this is by far the most powerful and enduring, indelibly etched in my consciousness.

This is the best gift I've ever received from anyone and I would like to pass that gift on to you.

Death brings us new perspectives on life, and so can birth. Both inextricably woven together in a cosmic play. I believe life takes on all sorts of different meanings when you begin to tap into having a purpose in life.

I vividly recall the day my first child was born. The moment I held her for the very first time and looked into her deep blue eyes, I instantly knew my life would never be the same. Suddenly, every ounce of my consciousness was transformed into much more than just being a husband, friend, co-worker, brother, or son. I became a Daddy!

In the blink of an eye, everything that was once important in my life became secondary to taking care of this little human being who was totally dependent on me for everything. My sense of purpose immediately became laser-sharp.

I'd waited until I was 43 to get married for the first time and two more years to welcome my first child, Jaycee. By then, I was pretty "stubborn", as my wife Tami tells me. When my son Colton came along two years later, it happened to me all over again! It happened yet again when my daughter Sierra was born seven years later.

The best part about kids is they don't care how much money you make, how expensive your car is, who you know, where you go on vacation, how good you are on PlayStation, or how far you can drive a golf ball. All they care about is being loved and spending time with you.

Since then, I have worked diligently to reinvent the ways that I put my life together, and how I approach what I do for a living.

In living a balanced life, I want to:

- Work smarter so I can spend more time doing OTHER THINGS!
- Work less so I can spend more time doing OTHER THINGS!
- Reinvent how I run my businesses so I can spend more time doing OTHER THINGS!

In essence, I want to work less and live more!

17

I've always approached my life like a bull in a china shop. But one thing I can say about my philosophy of Making Every Day a Saturday is that you only live this life once, so you'd better make it count!

The zeal for living that I've always possessed deep in my guts has fueled me for as long as I can remember. However, nothing compares to that feeling of sublime joy of having children. I still have a long list of passions and interests in my life, but my kids take the cake!

Now, I'm more determined than ever to not become a prisoner to my businesses, but to live life like I really mean it!

Recap:

- Treat every day like it's a Saturday.
- The most valuable asset that you have is your time and the most important decisions that you make are how you spend your time.

Chapter 2
Today's Unleashed Entrepreneurs (UEs)

Work less, live more.

Some people say I'm completely nuts. Others say I was born with a screw loose. Still others say that my approach to life doesn't mesh with being a traditional entrepreneur. In my defense, yep, that sounds just like me!

I am totally in love with what I do for a living, but I don't want to work anymore than I absolutely must to support the lifestyle I have built for myself. I have found that it's not necessary to spend unlimited hours immersed in my businesses to the point that I don't remember my kids' names, forget about the game, or that I needed to take the car into the mechanic for a tune-up. It's not worth it!

This book is written with the distinctive goal of giving "meat and potatoes" insights to the following types of people:

- Entrepreneurs who feel overwhelmed because their businesses have taken over their lives. I know the pain that comes from being in a rut. However, as a serial Lifestyle Entrepreneur, I can tell you that adversity being the mother of necessity can also propel you on to quantum leaps of self-improvement and prosperity.

- Wannabes with dreams of branching out on their own and starting businesses, to inspire them with behind-the-scenes glimpses from over three decades of creating, building, and running companies. Becoming an entrepreneur is truly one of the most deeply satisfying experiences you can ever have, and I would love nothing more than for you to get a fire under your butt to roll the dice and see what number comes up!

- Regular, older folks who want to increase the quality of their lives. This book contains golden nuggets that can give you a new set of eyes for what's truly important to enrich your life even more.

Whether you own a business or not, I call anyone who has a dream of placing their lifestyle before their job or business an **UNLEASHED ENTREPRENEUR (UE)**. Someone with the spirit and gumption to want a better life for themselves and their families.

I will share a vast plethora of cutting-edge business ideas, some counter-intuitive approaches to running a successful enterprise, and a few inspirational stories to illustrate important facts about living a passionate life as an entrepreneur in charge of your own destiny.

The bottom line is this: I want you to hand-craft the perfect life for yourself and your family, then work backwards and reverse-engineer your businesses to meet those goals. This book is a blueprint on how you can do this, too.

I've put in long days, long weeks, long months, and long years building brands that failed and succeeded. If you're in business, or thinking about taking the leap, that means you're not alone, and neither am I. We can learn from each other.

I did it for a distinct reason. It was all part of my master plan to create a phenomenal life. Over the course of my journey, I built successful brands that employed wonderful people, created needed products and services for my customers, and generated tremendous profits. It's wired in my DNA, and I love the steep climb!

What Is Your CORE?

There's an entrepreneurial flame deep inside my soul that never goes out. The voice in my head and heart urging me on, even when there is silence. This voice constantly instills in me the desire to make a profound difference in the world for the people that I call my CORE: my family, closest friends, and employees.

We all have this CORE group at the center of our universe. It's what gives us a distinctive reason to get up each day and put on our boots.

What are some of the reasons for starting your own business? Is it the joy of being a self-employed entrepreneur and dictating your own working hours? Or for the money? Is it the ability to dream your own dreams? Is it the ability to constantly breathe new life into your business creations, watching with bated breath, as it grows over time?

If you're a business owner, you're hopefully brimming over with the desire to become the very best you possibly can be. There is an innate desire deep inside each of us to reach for goals that seem unreachable. Some are lying just below the surface, but some have been deeply buried for so long, it will take time to dig them out. Maybe it's that dream you have of someday starting your own online marketing business, you put it aside until the perfect day because of kids, your job, or life's emergencies. Well, guess what? The stars will never line up completely, and there is never a better time than right now to jump in with both feet!

It's human nature to have something to gravitate to all the time and to keep striving for, but in today's world, it's easy to let our goals slowly slip into oblivion and become a distant memory if we aren't careful.

If someone asked us, we would readily acknowledge that we want life to be exciting, but some of us have gotten too comfortable and content sitting on our respective couches. We need a challenge, but only a few of us ever dare to follow our hearts. Are you ready to restart or start up your business?

Impassioned people put everything on the line to start their own businesses. However, the main reason is still that we have passion for what we do. The gardener who starts a nursery, a weekend barbecuer who opens a restaurant, a woodworker who starts a cabinet shop, or a photographer who opens a studio. We all share a common passion for what we do. There is absolutely nothing wrong with you wanting to monetize your passion and turn it into an actual job or business. That is the American Dream at full strength!

In the old days, the word *entrepreneur* meant someone who owned their own business, plus other not-so-sexy innuendoes. It also meant someone who worked long hours, didn't see and spend enough time with their family, risked everything they had to accomplish their goals, and lived on the edge between sanity and insanity.

Today, a new breed of amazing folks are breaking the old molds, creating their own rules, and blazing innovative new trails to pursue and attain their dreams with gusto and determination. There is a big tidal wave that is quickly sweeping the business world and it's a philosophy that is flipping traditional business models on their heads.

These UEs want to work less, play more, and redefine what it means to be a success.

They put their families and personal lifestyle choices first, then build their income blueprints based on these choices. In essence, this progressive trend exemplifies a reverse hierarchy of traditional business goal setting and what it means to have a successful brand.

To many traditional business owners, this type of thinking leads to doom and gloom. They ask, how can a business survive unless the ownership and management are willing to give up their souls to accomplish maximum profitability? How can anyone claim to be successful unless the business can scale to 10, 100, or 1000 employees and show doubling or tripling net profits year over year?

In my opinion, bigger isn't necessarily better. You will see examples of that throughout this book.

To a UE like myself, setting such outdated, outrageous goals today are secondary to attaining satisfaction from spending time with my family, personal projects, and rewarding lifestyle activities.

In my case, if something doesn't help me to attain my ultimate lifestyle goals, I take a pass on it.

Basically, if it's not a "HELL YES" then it must be a "BIG FAT NO!"

Your default answer to all new tasks or activities that require your attention must be NO. End of discussion. More on this later.

When I began thinking this way, I recalibrated the way that I approached creative problem solving and found innovative, out-of-the-box solutions.

Sadly, most people have no reason to think like this unless they are faced with a devastating event.

The goal of any successful marketer is find out how other businesses in your arena are operating, then don't do that! You want to run as fast as you can in the opposite direction and figure out ways to stand out in a crowded space. That is the sure-fire method of separating yourself from the rest of the pack!

I intentionally stay away replicating their structures, master marketing plans, and, most importantly, their systems. I've discovered this is one of the biggest killers of the entrepreneurial spirit because many systems are inefficient at best and self-destructive at worst. It kills many a dream.

Typically, many businesses are put together with the old-fashioned system of "business first, personal life last," which intrudes unforgivingly upon their owners' lives.

Why would I want to bring on pain in replicating the way these things are done? Most traditional businesses run on the upside-down pyramid that says your business is at the top of the food chain, with your lifestyle towards the bottom. That just doesn't make sense to me whatsoever.

This inverse strategy keeps my mind focused on priorities I value, while also giving me a focused, laser-like approach to getting my work done quickly and efficiently. This is how a true UE approaches creating something new and exciting.

I'm decorated with honor badges of trial-and-error, setbacks, and victories, but I've always been a willing participant in the process.

I've lived the better part of my life with this simple UE approach.

This book is going to show you how to attain your own levels of personal and business freedom with this perspective. It's not an easy move, but you'll NEVER want to go back to old-school rigmarole and stagnation when you make these changes.

Do you consider yourself as having an entrepreneurial spirit, regardless of whether you own a business? If you currently are a card-carrying member of the club, we are kindred spirits.

If not, maybe you know deep down that you are destined to become one of the chosen few.

I love Jeff Foxworthy and his "You Might Be A Redneck If" one-liners. They have become as American as apple pie and Chevrolet.

Well, you too might be an entrepreneur if:

- You have an insatiable desire to live a kick-ass life full of meaning and purpose.
- You get bored easily and can't stand wasting time.
- You have a deep motivation to overcome the odds, no matter how unlikely.

- You have an unbridled optimistic feeling about the world and your life, even when others around you ooze pessimism.

- You can't stand people wasting so much time with their faces buried in a device to the detriment of family and friends.

- You can't sit still.

- You prefer to break the rules instead of living within them.

- You stay away from low-energy people and their negative influences.

- You have an affinity towards risk-taking, small or large.

- Your favorite show is *The West Wing.*

- You have ideas rattling around in your head all the time and can't wait to try them out.

- You ask for forgiveness, instead of permission.

- You passionately study how winners operate to learn their secrets.

- You are constantly trying to learn new stuff.

- You have a hard time shutting down your brain at night or on weekends.

- You prefer reading nonfiction and informative how-to's to expand your knowledge base.
- You write your goals down on paper.
- You wish Robin Williams had made more movies.
- You have a "something shiny" syndrome where your attention span is extremely short.
- You feel like an outsider most of the time.
- You bounce back rapidly from failures and try again.
- You enjoy interacting with people smarter than you, so they inspire you.
- You work hard and play even harder!

If you answered yes to at least five of the above bullet points, I'm delighted to say that you are wired to be an Unleashed Entrepreneur, meaning we are cut from the same cloth!

If you answered yes to ten or more, you are officially a VIP member with a seat in the front row of life! Congratulations!

Recap:

- Work less, live more!
- Hand-craft your lifestyle, then reverse engineer your business.
- If it's not a hell yes, then it has to be a big fat no!

Chapter 3
What's Holding You Back?

How do you create a successful business that is unleashed and free from traditional, old-school rules? Well, you'll need to make some big decisions along the way and your entire approach to life may need a considerable overhaul. Your attitude and how you allocate the use of your time may also need to be recalibrated.

You'll have to learn to see life's journey as a wonderful roller-coaster ride filled with ebbs and flows, and, of course, heartaches.

You and I can surrender to circumstances in our life that always seem to come our way from day-to-day and live "a life of maintenance," or we can tap into our deepest sense of purpose so that peripheral circumstances won't matter.

Through the diverse variety of all my experiences, good and bad, I have come to this conclusion about the human spirit. We could probably all write a novel about opportunities that have come our way, and how we did absolutely nothing about them. We saw the opportunity but froze up under the pressure. *What if it doesn't work out? What if I fail? What if I make a fool of myself?*

Before long, we end up in a self-created prison that affects our entire life and emotions, including our family, physical health, and financial stability. We get so caught up in our outer circumstances we forget about our real life.

Let's say you get hit with some bad luck that limits your options. A bad day at work, a bad week, a bad month, an argument with a friend or your spouse, or some sort of financial dilemma can leave you with a bad year! Instead of dealing with it and moving on, many of us choose to let it bubble and fester, suppressing it to the point the world knows nothing about our situation. How dare life mess with our mojo!

Life is sometimes fair and quite often not. I can tell you one thing, though. People who work hard typically tend to have better luck in life.

Overcoming Obstacles, the Ultimate Expression

One of my favorite all-time artists is Billy McLaughlin, who makes the most fascinating sounds from an acoustic guitar.

Through the 1980s and 1990s, he was one of the best guitar players in the world, playing music like angels coming down from the heavens. He had devoted his life to his music and it showed!

In 1999, Billy began losing control on stage. At first, it was written off as a bad night. In 2001, he was diagnosed with "focal dystonia," an incurable neurological disorder. Years of dedication to his craft began to slip away. Billy continued to try with all his might to keep playing guitar, but there came a day when he was forced to quit.

By 2002, his career was over. I remember crying when I heard the news that he was done. Coming to terms with the diagnosis of dystonia was a monumental change for Billy and his outlook on life. In 2006, Billy attempted a comeback. He had been relearning his music and teaching himself to play all over again, note for note—*LEFT HANDED!*

It's not like walking backwards down the street or driving a car with the wheel on the opposite side. It's like learning to speak every word in reverse, phonetically! Focal dystonia took away Billy Mac's life as a musician—but his passion took it back!

I'm thrilled Billy Mac is once again inspiring audiences around the country with his unique music style. I've met many passionate people in my life, but none hold a candle to Billy Mac!

Be Passionate About EVERYTHING!

However, purpose and motivation don't strike us like lightning. These good habits must be cultivated through practice and patience. The exuberant enthusiasm that seeps from every cell of your body is not a feeling or a mood. You have to act.

Let's discuss some common deterrents preventing us from unleashing our potential as successful UEs.

Procrastination

I believe the biggest killer of our motivation and passion is procrastination. This unfortunate malaise is caused by our misunderstanding that doing certain tasks will cause us some sort of pain. Against that perceived pain, we must balance the enormous benefits.

Do any of these thoughts sound familiar?

- I'll get to it TOMORROW.
- I'll take the kids to the park NEXT weekend. I'll make that trip to Alaska when I retire.

- Maybe when I'm older.

- Perhaps when I'm more settled in my job.

- Maybe when the kids are out of the house.

- I'll buy that big TV I've been looking at for the last two years as soon as the old one breaks down.

What if that day never comes? No matter what your circumstances are in life, you will always come up with reasons why something can't be done. Instead, why not come up with one great reason why you should?

Procrastination can be the great robber of our time if we're not careful. Nothing will suck out the vigor for life faster than a good case of it. Show me a garage stuffed with *I'll get to it later* projects, and I'll show you a life that is not reaching its full potential. Nothing can stop a dream faster than our own laziness.

Well, today is the first day of the rest of your life! You can begin now to take control of your life and get back to that feeling of relevance and contentment.

Check out this piece of anonymous wisdom about procrastination:

They were going to be all that they wanted to be... tomorrow.

None would be braver or kinder than they... tomorrow.
A friend who was troubled and weary, they knew, would be
glad of a lift—and needed it too.
On him they would call—see what they could do... tomorrow.
Each morning they stacked up the letters they'd write...
tomorrow.
The greatest of people they just might have been, the world
would have opened its heart to them.
But, in fact, they passed on and faded from view, and all that
they left when their living was through was a mountain of
things they intended to do... tomorrow.

I can't impress enough upon you to take action today. If you can't see yourself realizing the dream, you never will. Just when you're about ready to succeed, something will surely pull you back. If you feel overwhelmed, break it down and get started!

After all, you can't eat an elephant all at once, can you? Start breaking down the big things in your life into small, manageable tasks to eat one bite at a time.

Ah, but there's always tomorrow, right?

Self-Doubt and Limited Ambition

Limited ambition is another obstacle to the UE life. Dreams should be just a little bit out of reach, but not out of sight. Otherwise, they wouldn't be dreams, would they? If your dreams exceed your self-image, you'll very likely do something stupid to sabotage that dream.

Earlier in my business life, I sabotaged many projects and got in the way of my own success. Ultimately, my self-doubt overwhelmed my desire to succeed. Once I learned to get out of my own way, my business fortunes changed.

Imagine when you wake up tomorrow, everything you do will be done to the best of your ability. You'll give 110% effort to each and every activity you've planned for your day, disregarding any fears you may have. No obstacles. No negative thinking. No procrastination.

How do you think this attitude will impact how your day turns out?

Resistance to Change

Resistance to change is another major obstacle that prevents us from leading an unleashed life. We're all creatures of habit, preferring to be comfortable with daily routines. Do you consider change wonderful and exciting, as long it's happening to someone else?

Life is in a constant state of flux, so we tend to gravitate towards our comfort zones. It seems too risky to try something new.

Comfort zones are neither good nor bad, but most people mistakenly think they perform their best when they are in a safe and familiar place.

I truly dislike being comfortable. If it gets to be too much, I'll create some chaos and shake up my world a bit. I get extremely bored with my life if my daily routines begin to feel "always the same." It drives me crazy to the point at which I must either create a new product, start a new business, buy a new business, or completely shake up my routines.

No matter how enthusiastic you are, you'll stagnate if you don't take responsibility in your job, marriage, friendships, and hobbies. Anything not making progress is on its way to becoming stagnant and boring, which is to be avoided when pursuing and embracing our lives with passion as successful UEs.

Now, I don't expect you to go to the extremes that I do when you get bored with your routines. Here are some exercises that can help shake the bushes of your life that may be easier to try:

- Try a new restaurant this week. I challenge you to try a cuisine you're unaccustomed to.

- Buy different brands at the grocery store, such as deodorant, toothpaste, or dish soap.

- Take a new route to work/from work you've never tried before. Be pleasantly surprised at how much beauty there is out there, if you give it a chance!

- Listen to a style of music you typically don't listen to. Scan your radio, download Amazon Music, or iHeartRadio. Give something new a try!

- Sample a different dinner recipe for seven straight nights. Google and research recipes, add the ingredients to your weekly shopping list, and give it a try. Give your culinary palate a shake up!

- Read a book completely out of your comfort zone.

- Switch the side of the bed you sleep on. You may have to sweet-talk your spouse or significant other, but you'll be amazed how different it makes you feel.

- If you have longer hair, try a different hair style or add some color.

- Pick an obscure subject you know very little about. Research and read about it, watch videos on it, then write a 500-word essay. Don't worry about making it sound like a Pulitzer prize-winning document, just pour your heart and effort into making it the best report you've ever written.

- Eat and write with your opposite hand for 24 hours. Don't worry about dropped spaghetti. Practice writing your name 25 times and see how much you can improve. This exercise activates the opposite side of your brain, rewarding you with a very powerful sensation after a short time. I try this technique 2-3 times a week, just to keep things a little off-centered.

- Instead of salting your food, try seasonings like salad dressings, hot sauces, pepper, BBQ sauces, vinegars, and spices for flavor. Make this a fun project and see what kinds of flavors stimulate your taste buds!

If you keep doing what you have always done, you'll keep getting what you've always gotten. It'll be virtually impossible to break out of your mental funk unless you shake up your mental branches to stimulate your foggy brain. I highly recommend trying at least some of these techniques over the coming days and weeks.

As Albert Einstein noted, "We cannot solve our problems with the same thinking we used when we created them."

Take a risk! You might not like it, but you'll never know unless you try.

If you step up to the plate, you might strike out. If you don't try, you'll never know the true joy of hitting a home run. Barry Bonds struck out over 1,500 times during his career, but he has also hit more home runs than anyone else in Major League Baseball history.

When you take a risk or face a fear, you move forward with your life. Eventually, you will become successful. As challenging as it may sound, this is a simple formula in living life to the fullest.

Here's another problem with comfort zones. If you're good, staying comfy can keep you from becoming great! That, in and of itself, should motivate you to get off your ass!

Lack of Discipline

Lack of discipline is another obstacle preventing us from living the UE life. Show me a successful businessperson, and I'll show you someone who is disciplined and dedicated to their mission.

Success and failure are habits and self-fulfilling prophecies. If you don't prioritize and build positive habits, you will just stagnate and create your own demise.

In high school, I competed in the 400 meters at the Junior Olympics and did very well on a national level for several years. Between my coach, parents, friends, and competition, I was able to create a very strong set of goals I wanted to accomplish with my running. At one point, my times were on track to qualify for the U.S. Olympic Trials in Eugene, Oregon. Unfortunately, a torn hamstring ended my college sprinting career, forcing me to retire long before I was ready.

But that experience left an indelible lifelong impact. Athletics is a powerful way to learn about self-discipline and setting goals. I know that my core values and beliefs are firmly rooted in the training I received from competitive sports.

Do you wait to see how you feel before making plans? Are you easily side-tracked or do you have a sense of discipline?

The key to staying focused and dedicated isn't hard if it's something you love and are passionate about.

Any discipline you desire must be built up gradually. If your goal is to run a marathon next year, you can't start out by running twenty-six miles on your first day of training. Start small and work your way up!

Fear

Our innate fear of trying something new has been part of human nature since the dawn of civilization. We tend to avoid any kind of risk if it has anything to do with taking us out of our comfort zone.

Fear stops many people from taking risks. If we aren't willing to walk out on a limb, we'll never get to the best fruit life has to offer.

Overcoming our fear is how you and I learned to do just about everything in our lives, such as eating different foods for the first time, driving a car, talking to strangers, speaking up at meetings, or playing catch with your kids. They all come with certain levels of risk.

Trying a new variety of apple vs. investing $1,000,000 into a new business are both risky in their own unique ways. As humans, we like to take "measured" risks, meaning we can mitigate what may happen to us.

Pessimists and negative thinkers say things like "You might get struck by lightning if you go outside," or "Did you know 103 people a day are killed in car wrecks in the US, which means I shouldn't drive?" Boy, what a waste of a person's great potential and mind space to think so negatively!

Nobody likes to lose, but there's no loss in going for it at all. The only loss in not trying is not having gone for it.

How do you overcome negative talk with yourself and people you meet? If you are unable to convince these people to be more open to having a positive outlook, then it's time to move on. Life is too short to allow yourself to be surrounded with people who attempt to bring you down, whether its unintentional or not.

It's completely cool to surround yourself with people who espouse ideas opposite to yours which can open your thinking to new ideas and creative problem solving, but negative thinking has no place in your 86,400-second day!

Recap:

- Instead of focusing on reasons why you can't do something, focus on the reasons why you should.
- Comfort zones can be the kiss of death in business.
- If you are good, comfort zones can prevent you from being great!
- There is no loss in going for it all, the only loss is in not going for it at all.

Chapter 4
Setting Goals

In my business life, I am ruthless. I'm an extremely aggressive marketer, an above-average salesperson who knows how to close, and I tend to find niches in the marketplace that are not being occupied by others. I know how to focus on my superpowers and squeeze out every drop of potential to win.

I delegate 80% of my daily tasks that brings only 20% of my results, leaving me with the 20% of my time to focus on the right tasks that bring 80% of my positive results. If you give me a brand-new business, I am confident that I will have that brand sailing towards the top of the food chain within six months. One of the biggest reasons this would happen is because I would offload what I would call the second-tier activities, which allows me to focus on getting the biggest return on my time investment.

I temper this confident attitude with a much more subdued approach to my personal life. Because I am dedicated to having my perfect lifestyle on top of the food pyramid, it makes me more dedicated to getting my work done as quickly and efficiently as possible.

In looking back on my business journey, my take to you is common sense. If you have a laser-beam focus on your goals, your priorities and time can allow you to revolutionize your business blueprint. My businesses are constrained by design. I have the mindset of a millionaire, but that doesn't mean that I must relinquish control over my life in order to attain that status.

Sharpening Your Focus

Once upon a time, a very big, strong woodcutter got a job working for a local business. The pay was great and so were the benefits. The woodcutter was excited and determined to do his absolute best to impress the boss. His boss gave him an axe and showed him the area where he was to work.

On the first day, the woodcutter brought back twenty-five trees.

"That's great," said the boss. "Keep up the good work!"

Totally motivated by his boss's encouragement, the woodcutter tried even harder the second day, but he could only bring back fifteen trees.

On the third day, he only brought back ten trees.

Day after day, he kept bringing back fewer and fewer.

"Something's wrong with me," the woodcutter surmised. "I'm losing my strength."

He went to the boss and apologized, saying he could not understand what was going on.

"When was the last time you sharpened your axe?" asked the boss.

"Sharpen?!" exclaimed the woodcutter. "I didn't have time to sharpen my axe. I have been too busy cutting trees!"

Are you keeping the edge of your axe sharp or have you been cutting trees blindly?

When was the last time you invested some time into learning a new skill or refining on an existing one? To get the most out of life, we must continue as professional students.

It's not about just setting goals for your business. Sharpening your focus means digging deeper to have a clearer understanding of what you really want out of life, what your true priorities are, and how to go about reaching those goals.

When you choose to stay focused on one single task at a time, you invariably end up cutting out some things you enjoy that may not be bearing fruit. We will do an exercise to help you eliminate, streamline, or delegate up to 80% of your daily tasks and free your time and energy to dedicate to your superpowers.

Most people have heard of the 80/20 Principle, which suggests that 80% of your outcomes are from 20% of your efforts. Conversely, 20% of your outcomes are from the other 80% of your efforts. The point here? Identifying a group of top priorities and then staying focused on them should be your #1 focus. I will deal with how you can figure this out in a later chapter, but for now I want you to begin thinking about what activities in your day produce the most amount of positive results in your business or personal life.

For many years, I made a fantastic living in the world of professional photography. Today, it seems like everybody and their brother's friend's aunt's sister is now a "photographer," which has put a big crunch on those who have been professionally trained. For example, "Weekend Warriors" and "Soccer Moms" have taken the industry by storm with their $500 cameras or smartphones.

Many professional photographers became slaves to their computers and workflows. Image processing that used to be handled by professional color labs are now being done by the photographers themselves, adding significantly more hours to their already long work week.

In photography, only three things make money: shooting, selling, and marketing. That's it! Retouching a digital file doesn't fall under any of those categories, but many pros are being consumed by this digital process. Why? Because they think it saves money, and they know how to do it. A deadly combination.

It doesn't bother us to dispose of things we dread and despise, but what if they were things we're attached to? This makes it a lot harder because our emotions are involved. Photographers who spend eight hours on a Sunday editing and retouching files from Saturday's wedding are attached to an outdated method of running a business.

Instead of outsourcing the job to someone to free up their valuable time, they choose to do it themselves because they're emotionally attached to the digital process or mistakenly think they're saving money.

I can tell you this without any hesitation. $10-$15 per hour work is NOT what business owners should be doing with their time, whatever industry they're in!

Do you have a list of tasks that can be delegated or eliminated from your routine? Think about that.

This way of thinking may be counter-intuitive to the way you have been used to thinking during most of your working career, but I can tell you your business will be revolutionized by quantum leaps if you begin to entertain the idea of redesigning your thought processes.

Let's proceed with a simple exercise that will start defining some of your personal and professional goals, which will ultimately lead to the master plan for your perfect lifestyle. Don't worry about the money aspect for now. Just answer these questions honestly. Let your mind expand and play as much as you like.

It may feel a little awkward at first, but that's okay. Have fun playing and imagining your dream lifestyle.

If you had a magic wand:

- How many days off a week would you like?
- What will you do with your free time?
- Where would you like to travel?
- What hobbies would you like to spend more time on?
- What kind of car do you want to drive?

- What kinds of clothes do you want to wear?

- What kind of house do you want to live in?

- Which relationships are most important to you, and how can you nurture them?

- What would you change about yourself for self-improvement?

We'll call this perfect lifestyle list the Holy Grail since it contains all the shiny objects in the sky you'll always be striving for as an UE.

Be sure to write down your answers. Simply writing down your thoughts and goals is more effective in communicating with your subconscious to better achieve your aspirations.

Now, here is the challenging part. You need to come up with a grand total dollar amount. How much will it take to comfortably sustain your vision for the Holy Grail? You have now started to paint a picture of your perfect lifestyle.

Deciding on what you want is the all-important first step towards getting it. Our thoughts determine the direction of our lives.

Life is more about the journey than the destination. If you change your thinking, you can change your life.

Harness Your Mental Power to Imagine Success

Imagine a big, juicy lemon sitting on the table in front of you. A large, yellow lemon just sitting there looking up at you.

Grab a knife and cut it into wedges, the juices squirting all around as you slice into the skin. With your mind's eye, smell the citrusy aroma wafting through the room. The refreshing scent fills the air with bursts of new energy to revitalize your senses. Still in your mind's eye, take a wedge, take a huge bite, and suck the wedge until all the juice is completely in your mouth.

Are you salivating? This is how the power of words affects and engages us emotionally. Words are simple tools that enable us to create dreams, including that amazing vision of where you want to be in your life.

Do you have a vision of how you want your life to be? Is your dream embedded in your brain in a way that is so compelling that it drives you to where you need to be? Is it as compelling as the cut lemon and refreshing aroma wafting through all your senses?

Your mind is an incredibly powerful tool in helping you achieve goals and grab your slices of happiness.

We've been taught to believe our dreams are not meant to come true and that dreaming takes us away from tasks at hand. People accused of being daydreamers are thought to be lazy, foolish, or "not plugged into reality."

And yet, how would things have ever gotten done if we didn't imagine the results beforehand? If Thomas Edison had not tried, failed, and retried over 6,000 times, we would not have the benefit of electric lightbulbs today.

Despite its negative reputation, daydreaming, is key to sharpening your focus on what you really want. Every invention and every great new idea was birthed at one time by people who "daydreamed." I've been accused of being a daydreamer for much of my life, but I can honestly say that many of my "aha!" bright ideas have been the result of my mind being allowed to wander off into the great unknown.

Once upon a time, there was a man living in a cold cave who daydreamed about making fire to stay warm, but it took us over one million years to figure out how to utilize it. Someone daydreamed about inventing ice cream over 4,000 years ago, but it wasn't until only over a hundred years ago that someone came up with the idea for the ice cream cone. In 1775, the flush toilet was invented, followed 82 years later by the invention of toilet paper!

The world goes around because of people who daydreamed, imagined, and strongly believed they could make the world a better place for themselves and others.

You're never too young or too old to dream big dreams. Figure out what's holding you back from designing the life of your dreams and then forge ahead.

Taking Responsibility

We have all had times when we felt like the world was out to get us. I remember events in my life when it seemed everything I was doing didn't turn out as planned, regardless of how hard I tried. I felt I was doing the right things with the right amount of effort, but the dice just didn't roll my way.

Looking back at every one of my failures, I can say with 110% certainty that the reason I failed was because of my attitude and my effort.

There was a time in my life when I made terrible financial decisions, leading to my filing for bankruptcy back in the 1990s. It was a difficult lesson, but one I wouldn't trade for anything in the world. Without this failure, I wouldn't have been able to lay the groundwork for future successes and accomplishments. I had to take responsibility for my bad decisions and live with the consequences.

It wasn't my potential that caused me to fail. If that was the case, my entire life would be filled with nothing but outright winning.

If you ask a successful businessperson about lessons they learned from failing, they will be able to tell you countless stories in excruciating detail. However, hitting the bottom does teach us many lessons, one of which is you don't want to be there ever again!

How many times have you heard, "Oh, you have so much potential." You can die from a terminal case of potential!

Taking responsibility is the match that sets passion afire. We must want to have a better attitude in life so passion can arise from the depths of our guts to fill out every cell of our being. Conversely, a bad, negative, and pessimistic attitude kills passion and needs to be exterminated ASAP!

Uncaring people with bad attitudes are always unhappy and they can't understand why. Do you know anyone with that kind of mentality? Maybe they spend too much time talking about all the cool TV shows they watch every day or spend all their time keeping up with everyone else's business. Worse, they spend every waking moment with their faces buried in their devices as life passes them by. If this is you, YOU NEED TO STOP!

To live the life of a UE, you must avoid becoming stagnant, inactive, and prevent yourself from getting a terminal case of "bad attitude." If you've lost the joy on your life's journey, maybe it's because you've allowed a bad attitude to creep into your head space. You must take responsibility for allowing this to happen, however unconsciously it may have occurred.

To me, "attitude" is much more important than your background, education, money, failures, successes; or what other people think, say, or do. If all but one of the strings on your guitar is broken, then all you can do is play on that one string that's left: your attitude. I'm convinced life is 5% of stuff happening to me, and 95% how I react to it.

How prepared are you to meet adversity? What percentages would you use to describe how you react to circumstances?

Moreover, it's very easy for entrepreneurs to fall into that old management trap of getting caught up in the daily grind of managing our businesses. It sucks up the energy, time, and motivation to enjoy happy moments we feel we're owed, such as daydreaming and designing your perfect lifestyle.

Managing employees, refining your website SEO, crafting your social media posts, keeping up with marketing and promotions, cleaning the bathroom, mowing the lawn, and doing the books can be too rigorous for one person. Before we know it, we're working sixteen hours a day, week after week.

For what?

Scarily and sadly, we don't have time for our families. We don't have time to play with our kids, drop a fishing line, hit that golf ball up and down the fairway, or watch our favorite shows. Things that are most important to us start slipping away gradually and unbeknownst to us, we have become enslaved to our business, instead of being master of our own kingdoms.

Private Time and "Popcorning"

Spending time with nobody else around is the foundation of all successful entrepreneurs, regardless of what industry they are involved in. Without private time, you will find it next to impossible to realize your full potential and set yourself on the path that leads to the proper work/life balance.

When I get bored or want to give myself a jolt of creative electricity, I go to the mountains in Montana. Simple things like listening to the sounds of the wind dancing through the tall trees, watching the morning mist rise from the wet grass and river, and building a campfire with while having a good cup of coffee are euphoric and revitalizing to me.

There are trees and rivers in every corner of the country, but Montana has a special power over my soul. Pat and my mother bought property there back in the 1990s. It is a nurturing place making me feel most at home, regardless of where I live.

Mother Nature is the battery for my soul. I can easily get in touch with myself very quickly in her midst. Regardless of what is going on in my life, she always puts things back in order and gives me the proper perspective to solve many of life's problems.

I don't really have to travel to Noxon, Montana to connect with myself. At times, I simply go out to our motorhome in the driveway or on the back deck. It's all a matter of perspective!

Once upon a time, a big dreamer named Walt Disney sat down with a group of intelligent businessmen to describe his vision of building the best theme park in the world! As he described his vision of a place he called Disneyland, he said he already knew the man whom he wanted to direct the project. Disney didn't know his name, but he knew that he was the man who put the United States Navy back in the Pacific Ocean after Pearl Harbor was bombed.

Disney's staff scoured the country to find Admiral Joe Fowler, who came to Walt Disney's office to listen about Walt's vision for a theme park.

"Do you understand who I am?" Admiral Fowler laughed. "I just won World War II and you want me to work for a guy who draws cartoons for a living?"

Walt wouldn't take no for an answer even though Joe kept saying that he was retired.

Finally, Walt's persistence paid off and Joe began to see his dream. At the young age of 56, Joe Fowler started an entirely new career and oversaw the building of Disneyland.

You may think that's the end, but it's only the beginning. Many years later, Walt Disney approached Joe again to build Disney World. Once again, Disney's clear vision was so compelling that Joe Fowler built Disney World at the age of 77.

Ten years later, Walt Disney approached Fowler with the plans for Epcot Center. By this time, Joe's attitude had changed a tad.

"You don't have to die until you want to," he said.

Here's an endearing message for us all to cherish. Joe had no idea when his time would be up, but he took responsibility for living every minute to the fullest!

Whenever you feel stuck or just spinning your wheels, the best thing you can do is to spend private time and be alone for a while. Dive deep into the depths of your soul. Call upon your inner pilot to figure out how to meet challenges and to overcome obstacles.

We all have a reservoir of passion welled up inside. It boils down to finding out how to turn on the spigot! The process is different for each of us. Once you discover how to turn the tap on, figure out the steps that allowed you to do this and do it over and over again!

To set constructive sights on your future, you must have a vision of where you want to go. After all, we drive with our focus towards safely reaching our destination, not on the highway passing below us.

My favorite story about focusing on your inherent talent comes from Lewis Carroll. As Alice was walking through Wonderland, she came to a fork in the road and met the Cheshire cat.

"Which road do I take?" Alice asked.

"Well, where do you want to go?" asked the Cheshire cat.

"I don't know."

"Then any road will get you there."

Recap:

- You need to have a laser-beam focus on your goals and priorities.
- $10-$15/hour work is not how business owners should be spending their time.
- Don't be satisfied with less.
- Don't become stagnant.
- Don't settle for good enough.
- Life is more about the journey than it is about the destination.
- Taking responsibility is the match that sets passion afire.

Chapter 5
What Motivates You?

Being successful is a huge motivator for any UE. I assume your drive to succeed is incredibly strong and you put tremendous value into the power of your dreams. Through hard work and sheer determination, your dreams gradually begin to take on a palpable life of their own. The brain is an amazing thing!

You work hard day in, day out, building and creating your brand, while providing wonderful goods and services to the world, employing workers, all of which pay you back with a feeling of accomplishment for a job well done.

Taking an idea and breathing life into its belly, then watching it become something you and the world can be proud of gives you an incredible high. Anyone who owns a business undoubtedly has a list of personal motivators to continue staying motivated, and to keep on working smarter.

As we discussed earlier, success is a relative term and varies from person to person. It's not always connected to how much revenue you generate or how many employees you have. It's a definition that each of us arrive at individually based on our goals, dreams, and lifestyle vision. It's all a matter of perspective!

Life's Great Lesson

One day, a millionaire businessman took his son to the country to show him how the poor folks lived. They spent a few days on a farm with an extremely poor family that didn't have a fancy car, an extravagant home, or even the extra money to be able to go out to dinner now and then. After they returned home, the father asked his son what he thought of his experience.

"It was great, Dad," the son replied.

"Did you see how poor some people in this world are?" the father asked.

"I sure did. I saw that we have a dog, and they have four. We have a big pool in our backyard and they have a lake and a stream running through theirs that has no end. In our garden, we have fancy imported Italian oil lamps, and they have a sky filled with the stars. Our patio reaches all around to our front porch, and they have the entire horizon. Thank you, Dad, for showing me how poor we really are."

What a great lesson for all of us. Life is totally a matter of perspective, and this boy nailed it!

Some people think that their value as a human being comes from working long hours, driving big expensive cars, dropping $50K on a vacation, and having lots of bling.

Me, I'm more of a barbecue on the back deck, guitar in the corner, hanging out in the mountains, reading a good business book, and playing with my kids. That's not to say that I don't enjoy the finer things in life, but we all need to stick to our core values and beliefs.

Love from Your Heart

Real love is a big motivator for me. I'm not talking about the kind of love you have for a double cheeseburger with fries, rooting for your favorite sports team, or a good book.

I'm talking about pure, unadulterated, unconditional love that can only come from a pure heart. If you're a parent, you know exactly what I mean. The kind of love that propels you to do anything to make sure your children are safe, protected, and cared for.

My grandparents were married for over fifty years before my grandmother passed away. Every time I saw them together, they held hands as if it were the first time they met. It made my heart melt.

I waited until I was in my forties to marry for the first time. The very instant my kids were born, my motivations immediately changed. Suddenly, my thoughts turned to becoming a phenomenal dad, a compassionate husband, and a world-class entrepreneur who had a laser-like focus on building my brands.

In many respects, I grew up each time to become even more responsible as soon as I saw the precious faces of my children at their births. My motivations and attitude towards what I was doing with my life had changed.

Some people are motivated by doing good for others, but others are happy to simply bring a smile to someone else's face.

However, people can also be motivated by negative factors, such as revenge, bitterness, jealousy, insecurity, or fear, too. These are not healthy reasons for you to do anything, and hopefully you don't have them anywhere in your "Top 40" list.

Positive or negative motivators are the very fuel for our cars to drive us safely along life's highway. These forces drive us every day, and it's important to have a handle on what makes us tick and gives us inspiration.

Some of these inspirations come from powerful moments that you experience.

When kids are little, you can tell them just about anything and they'll believe you, regardless of how far-fetched the concept is. Sasquatch lives in the forest behind your house; eating your carrots makes you see through walls; your parents are the smartest people in the world. Of course, this truism shatters when they turn twelve, when they discover they know everything!

Every parent has lists of "stretched truths" they tell their children. They serve as comical relief in an otherwise treacherous job of raising little humans who will someday rule the world.

When my oldest daughter Jaycee was about three, I jokingly told her that I was seven. To a youngster who doesn't have a grasp of concepts like time or age, this is a huge number that's very believable. She didn't know anyone who was that old since it wasn't a subject that regularly came up. I would occasionally remind her during the year I was seven, and it became part of our virtual reality as a family.

Well, my next birthday came, and I turned eight. The next year, I turned nine. By that time, Jaycee began learning about things that were tied to being a certain age like TV show ratings, driving privileges, and alcohol consumption. We would sit down to watch a movie on Friday Night Family Date Night. If the movie was PG or PG-13, she'd say, "Daddy, we can't watch this movie because you aren't old enough."

To keep my cover, I'd look at my wife, and begrudgingly finding a different movie for my age range. As for driving and alcohol, I said "they" gave me a special license to drive, and if you were 150 pounds, that allowed you to drink. This worked. I was able to squeeze more time out of my gig.

When I turned twelve, my house of cards came crashing down.

One day, Jaycee and I drove to the store alone.

"Daddy, do you know what's really weird?" she said. "You're twelve. I have classmates with brothers and sisters who are twelve. You're a lot bigger than them. That's really weird!"

My brain began to figure out a creative way to get out of this bind. Something ingenious to tell my grandkids later, that smacked of pure joy, unadulterated humor.

I looked back at her with a completely straight face, crafting the perfect comeback that was going to change the future of fatherhood, forever. She looked at me with her curious, confused eyes waiting for me to speak. And then...

I had nothing. Nothing at all!

"Honey, Daddy has a secret to tell you, but you have to promise not to tell your brother," I said. "I'm not twelve."

Her face turned to complete and utter confusion as she tried to ponder what that meant. I'd just shattered one of her deepest belief systems, and she didn't know how to deal with it. I felt closer to her at that moment than I had ever in her entire life because I was about to tell her one of my deepest, darkest secrets.

"Daddy isn't twelve," I continued. "He's fifty-two."

Total silence. More silence. Followed by even more deadening silence. I knew she was trying to think if she knew anyone that old in her mind. The pin-drop moment lasted for what seemed like an eternity. She spoke words I'll never forget for the rest of my life.

"Does Mommy know you aren't twelve?" she asked.

"I don't know, baby girl, but let's keep it a secret just between us, okay?" I replied, barely keeping it together.

71

"You also have to promise me you won't tell your brother either, since he doesn't know yet."

Every time the family hung out and the subject of birthdays or age came up, we'd look at each other and exchange small winks, then go back to what we were doing. This continued for a few weeks.

One day, Jaycee just had to know if Mommy knew my true age.

"Do you know Daddy isn't twelve?" she whispered.

My wife Tami looked at her and nodded. From then on, this special one-of-a-kind Daddy-daughter moment was officially over.

Within the next year, my son made the same realization, and we had a similar bonding moment when he discovered my real age.

Now, I have started the process all over again with my three-year old daughter. In her mind, I'm six-years old! I can tell you one thing for sure. I will enjoy every moment of the next several years until the magic melts away.

Precious moments such as these can recalibrate our perspectives and how we live our life. I don't want to miss a single magical moment.

It took me many years to arrive at my mind-boggling epiphanies that caused me to reinvent the way my businesses are built from the ground up. I used to be that guy who would put in 80 hours at the office in order to attain "the American Dream", but now my definition has morphed into something completely different. Now, I build brands based on what my lifestyle choices are.

What life-altering moments are motivating you?

Recap:

- Motivators, both positive and negative, are the very fuel for our cars to drive us safely along life's highway.
- Moments in your life can help recalibrate your perspective and how you live your life.

Chapter 6
The Perfect Day

Life is much more than working fifty years, putting a boatload of money in the bank, and hoping you're healthy enough to enjoy your retirement years. This concept is mistakenly engineered into our socio-economic-cultural fiber. We continue to perpetuate this dysfunctional thinking to our children, and on to our children's children.

When I was young, all I heard from people were snippets such as these:

"Work your ass off until you are 65. Put part of every paycheck into savings for when you retire. Don't waste your money on expensive cars or eat at fancy restaurants because that money should be saved for retirement. Don't take long, far-away vacations because they reduce the amount of money you have for retirement savings."

We've been hoodwinked into believing we must delay enjoying our happiness and set ourselves up for a cushy lifestyle, but only after we're done working.

Yet, unfortunate things do happen. Our bodies break down much faster than anticipated, our careers never go exactly as planned, and bad things happen along the way. We have absolutely no idea what the world is going to be like tomorrow, let alone 30-50 years from now.

We're asked to forgo life's revitalizing pleasures while young-in exchange for a few years of "old-age bliss." Come on! When we may not be able to see, or may not be able to move around like we did when we were younger? Yet we still blindly go about our daily lives in "working towards retirement," which may or may not ever come!

I say you can live like a king today, in living the life of your dreams starting today, with just a little creative thinking, old-fashioned ingenuity, and the willingness to try new ideas. There's no need to sacrifice receiving rewards that are rightly due to you now.

It's not about spending an ungodly amount of money either. As we've discussed, it's all a matter of perspective.

I like to call each weekend a "mini-retirement" and try to partake in activities that free my mind from stresses of my work week. I try to cram as many things into those 48 hours as is humanly possible. And if there were ever a 3- or 4-day weekend, WATCH OUT, WORLD!

If we want to make every day a Saturday, we should learn to live a life of "mini-vacations" or "mini-retirements" to recharge and reenergize our batteries. In fact, I challenge you to have a mini-retirement this weekend!

Like Abraham Lincoln cautioned, "And in the end, it's not the years in your life that count, it's the life in your years."

Set Your Personal Goals Now!

A potter knows that to end up with something worthwhile, they must know ahead of time what they're making. If you simply threw the lump of clay onto the potter's wheel without knowing what you wanted to make, you'd end up with the same lump. You must have an idea of what you're trying to accomplish-before you begin the process of formation and transformation.

Likewise, the caterpillar's calling to become a butterfly means it must strain, grow, stretch, and change within the confines of its chrysalis. Before it emerges from its sheltered cocoon to fly away, the caterpillar must struggle and strain to get out of its prison and fulfill its destiny. It's a struggle of a process to grow and mature. That's similar to why you're not meant to stay inside a cocoon forever.

You're meant to fly!

With that said, the process of imagining "a perfect lifestyle" can give us leeway to craft "a perfect day."

Start With The End, And End With The Beginning.

Let me tell you what a perfect day is for me.

I would wake up at 4:00 AM, feeling refreshed physically and emotionally. After spending time outside with our dog Tilly, I'd enjoy a fresh-brewed cup of French Roast coffee with half-and-half and honey.

The table next to my recliner is piled high with books/magazines that I'm ecstatic to dive into. I'd have some new-age jazz, classic rock, or a podcast playing away in my ears. Once I checked my sports scores, the news, and weather for the day, I'd spend the first two hours immersed in self-improvement activities to get my juices flowing. All private time with no interruptions.

The next hour would be spent in the REFLEX ZONE responding to the world's requests for my time. I'd reply to emails, honey-do lists, and other activities centered around the demands on my time from outside sources.

After that, I'd wake my kids from their night's slumber and help them get ready for their day. With kids ranging from ages three to twelve as I write this book, each has their own unique morning rituals and personality traits. They have different start times for school, allowing me the chance to converse with them individually. It's a precious way of getting to know them just a little bit better with daddy-bonding time before the day began for us.

I send each off to school with the biggest hug in the world, and an amazing affirmation of, "I LOVE YOU TO MARS AND BACK TIMES INFINITY PLUS 10!" They know beyond a doubt their Daddy loves them more than any other Daddy has ever loved their kids.

My wife Tami and I would have a tremendously engaging and productive morning meeting, talking about everything from our kids and family plans to the agenda for our work day. Just a nice slice of time with my wife talking about life!

Then, time to go to work. During my pre-planned work hours, I'd be uber-efficient with my responsibilities, such as making calls, writing projects, team meetings and training, product evaluations, recording podcasts, and other business activities.

All these activities would be put into what I call a "POD." In my definition, it means a section of time dedicated to a singular task or series of similar tasks without the influence of outside forces.

I want to have the best time anyone can legally have while working. Remember, I love what I do so much that I believe I haven't worked a single day since the spring of 1994, so it's very easy for me to imagine this. Short, sweet, and to the point. I would get maximum results for minimal amounts of effort expended.

Work time done, back to the fun!

There'd be a fishing pole and a pack of night crawlers waiting for me as soon as I'm done working, I'd spend an hour catching the biggest trout you ever saw! The fish would put up a great fight before finally being defeated by my outstanding fishing skills. On the way home, I'd have inspiring phone conversations with my Mom, my Dad, and my best friend, Mark.

By the time I got home, the kids would be getting off the school bus. I'd proceed to hear about their day's activities and help them with homework.

We would then adjourn to the kitchen to prepare a delicious 5-course meal, each member of the family preparing a course, that would fit in with a chosen culinary theme.

After dinner, a family board game or some guitar playing, playing with our dog Tilly, listening to my twelve-year-old play her flute, watch my son's hermit crab, or play dungeon with my three-year-old. Laughing until my sides hurt, then more laughing.

After shower and reading time, it's to bed for all the munchkins while reviewing our day together. I try to squeeze just a few more minutes and moments of happiness out of them.

Then, I'd head downstairs to finish up with any incomplete projects for the day, spend time with Tami, and cap it all off with a relaxing sauna and a hot shower. Lastly, I'd read in bed until I slowly drift off into slumber for the night.

What a perfect day that would be! All my favorite people and experiences rolled up into a single day.

Does it sound too simple? Maybe.

Then again, I can tell you that it happens on a regular basis in my life. I have a perfect day ALL THE TIME!

I call these type of perfect days "LEVEL I" days. It's a day I love replicating repeatedly, and they have become the cornerstone of my own perfect lifestyle. Such days are filled with the people and things I love and outcomes I can anticipate. Do these days have setbacks and surprises? Absolutely. But I try to be flexible and roll with the adversity and unexpected surprises.

If I keep the big picture in mind, the perfect day seems to work itself out, even with occasional bumps along the road. My bar is set at a level where I know I can be successful consistently, instead of setting myself up for failure.

All too often, people set the bar so high that it would take a few miracles to achieve success at any level. It makes much better sense to reward yourself with mini-victories along the way, doesn't it?

I have other type of Perfect Days as well.

LEVEL II includes achievable goals, events, and experiences that can't be replicated every day, such as:

- Watching a championship game with any of my teams playing, such as the LA Dodgers, Angels, Lakers, USC Trojans, UCLA Bruins, LA Kings, Colorado State Rams, Gonzaga Bulldogs, the Arkansas Razorbacks, or

John Daly the golfer. Unfortunately, many of my teams don't make it to their respective championship games, but I'm a true fan. I hurt for days, even weeks when we lose a tough game. But I keep the dream alive 365 days a year! Sports fans, you know exactly what I'm talking about. Win or lose, we're their biggest fans!

- Attending a concert for one of my favorite artists.
- Spending a holiday celebration with my immediate family.
- Launching a new product or service for one of my companies.
- Giving a seminar to a large group of hungry entrepreneurs and hearing about their successes.
- Spend the entire day in a workshop networking with other like-minded UEs.
- Hitting annual sales projections.
- Taking the motorhome on a mini-vacation to the mountains and finding a secluded spot.

LEVEL III perfect days are goals, events, and experiences that require extensive planning, discipline and commitment, such as:

- Hanging out on the beach in Mexico for a month without a single thing to do except eat and scuba dive.

- Taking a month off with the motorhome and living in the mountains, waking up every morning to the sound of a rushing river and singing birds.

- Buying or selling a business.

- Being with my kids when they reach lifetime milestone markers, such as their first steps, first day out of diapers, first straight-A report cards, first time driving, graduation, weddings, and the birth of every grandchild.

I could go on for an entire chapter listing the different types of perfect days, but I think you get the point.

These are individual, single events happening in life, but I have created the vision in my mind of how a perfect day can be built around these activities. I want to have perfect days all the time! I work hard to keep that vision strongly embedded in my brain.

I want my life to be filled with the best days ever, one right after the next. I don't mind meeting and overcoming setbacks that stand in the way because I know the best things in life require a little pain on occasion.

You may look at my day as a simpleton at work, and I thank you for the compliment! I am passionate about the pursuit of happiness in my life and that has become the cornerstone to my definition of what a perfect day means to me. I suggest you seriously consider this core idea for your emotional health and the health of your business.

We each have a different interpretation of our ideal lifestyle and that is great. Your day is unique to you and nobody else in the universe.

I truly believe I can have perfect days. I also truly believe you can experience them as well.

Does this sound counter-intuitive to the way you're used to setting goals or taking on challenges? To truly live the unleashed life, this step is a vital piece to the puzzle as you'll discover.

Our lives are made up of dreams, goals, aspirations, wants, desires, and unmitigated passions. Many of us may talk a good game, but we tend to fumble the ball on the five-yard line when it comes to the follow-through.

Don't feel bad if this sounds like you. The world is full of people who have a difficult time finishing what they start. It's very easy to get side-tracked or lose focus on the goals we have set, especially with endless forces vying for your time and attention. The sad part is we have allowed our time to be hijacked right in front of our very eyes.

Success is achieved with a series of mini-steps that will ultimately take you to the finish line.

You're basically planning and working backwards with your entire life, which will then give you the vision of what needs to get done.

Let's say that tomorrow you can have the best day of your life. No rules, no limitations. When you go to bed tonight, you know tomorrow upon waking up that this ideal day is truly happening. Would that change your perspective on how you approached the day?

Crafting Your Perfect Day

Before we begin, when was the last time you remember having a day like this? How many perfect days have you had over this past week, month, or year? How do they make you feel? Are you having a tough time coming up with answers quickly?

As we create your "Holy Grail Day," you'll need to consciously try not to let emotions and routines get in your way of building your new house. We're bulldozing your current lifestyle all the way down to the foundation, throwing out your preconceived notions of what total contentment means to you, and rebuilding a much better frame.

To begin, ask the following questions, reflect on your answers, and write them all down.

- What would your perfect day look like to you?
- What activities would you do?
- Where would you go?
- Who would accompany you?
- What kinds of food would you eat?
- What music would you play in the background?
- How would you volunteer/give back to community in any way?
- What new skill would you learn?
- Most importantly, how would this special day make you feel?

- Is this a feeling you want to experience more of in your life?

- Is this day achievable and realistic?

- Can you create this day within the structure of your current life? I'm hoping you give it an emphatic yes!

You now have created the Holy Grail Day on paper for yourself, and that's a pretty big deal in my book!

Let's stretch out this exercise and turn your perfect day into the perfect lifestyle! Would you do the same things or add some additional ingredients to your recipe? Do NOT allow yourself to feel guilty because you are indulging yourself. This is YOUR time, and nobody can tell you otherwise. Keep in mind what your overall lifestyle goals are while you're doing this.

Please write down all of it, either in your journal or on note cards filed away in a shoebox. Everything from A-to-Z. Let your imagination run wild and your pen run out of ink.

- Where would you live?

- What kind of house would you have?

- What kind of car would you like to drive?

- Where would you go on vacation?

- What new projects/businesses would you start?

- What workshops or courses would you attend?

- What nonprofit/charity help would you like to do?

- How would you give back to your community in kind and/or money?

- How much money would you set aside for retirement, second homes, college tuitions, a private jet, property in Montana, or whatever else you might want?

Allow yourself to have the creative freedom to authentically set these aspirations and goals. Unless you dream it, you'll never achieve it!

Ask yourself these and many more questions as you slowly create your masterpiece. Maybe you are already living the perfect life and that is very possible. To you, I say congratulations and a job well done. If not, we have a little more work to do. Make sure you are writing down your thoughts and answers.

Now the tough question. To make this life possible, what kind of income would you need to generate from your job, business, or both?

If you've already achieved this number, congratulations! You are the proud owner of the perfect lifestyle and you didn't even know it. You are now one step closer to living the life of your dreams.

But if that number is beyond where you are now with your income you'll need to reverse-engineer and restructure your business to attain your perfect life.

This book is not about different ways to generate money for your lifestyle (investments, passive income, real estate, stocks, growing your business, etc.). I assume you come to this book with a firm grasp on your finances. This is a book about putting value in your dreams, getting control of your time, and crafting a better life for yourself and your family while running a profitable business.

Now you have some guidelines for what you would like your life to look like from close range and from a distance.

Recap:

- Perception is the foundation for all human experiences.
- And in the end, it's not the years of your life that count, it's the life in your years.
- You are not meant to stay inside a cocoon forever. You are meant to fly!
- Build your life so you can experience a perfect day all the time!
- The best things in life require a little pain.
- Setting the bar so high that it would take a miracle to achieve success is a mistake. you should reward yourself with mini-victories along the way.
- Success is a series of mini steps that will ultimately take you across the finish line.
- Unless you dream it, it will never achieve it.

Chapter 7
The 24/7 Mentality

Do you think an astronaut could fly a spaceship to the Moon without studying hard and embarking on a disciplined physical training regimen? Could a surgeon perform open-heart surgery without going to school for many years? Can you become a world-class entrepreneur simply by hanging up your shingle and printing out business cards? Not in a million years!

To build a profitable business doing what you love absolutely requires a dream, hard work, and determination, as well as an understanding of the inner-workings of your personal DNA.

When you hear "24/7," what do you immediately think of? Most people think of 24 hours a day, 7 days a week. This typically refers to someone who keeps their nose to the grindstone all the time or a business that never closes, right?

Does this sound like anyone you know? I believe this describes a very large population in the world these days.

However, my definition of the 24/7 work mentality is quite different. To me, it means 24 hours a week, 7 months a year.

Let that soak in a minute.

Some of my business activities are seasonal, which requires me to put in very long days to have the lifestyle I've chosen for myself and my family. I've decided not to spend a majority of my time and energy in work-type operational activities.

I understand the actual demands that a thriving business places on your time, creative juices, and attention, but wouldn't it be wonderful if you kept this type of approach as your "dangling carrot" that you constantly strive for? It would allow you to constantly look for ways to streamline your workload, reduce the amount of wasted motions spent in your business, and to focus your attention on what generates the most positive results.

I'm against my businesses consuming my heart and soul at the expense of personal enrichment and family time. It's not worth it, even on my worst day! Life is too short for that.

You may think it's a bit of a "pie in the sky" dream, but I keep that at the forefront of my thinking. On some weeks, I'm not successful, but it's my dream to have that lifestyle and I work every day to make the dream come true.

The 24-Hour Tracking Assignment

Something very beneficial and revealing is to track your time for a 24-hour period. For everything you do, write it down. You could create categories like eating, personal grooming, reading, social media (a big one!), phone calls, marketing, selling, family time, personal time, and so on. Check and mark down every minute as much as possible and see where you end up at the end of the day. You'll be surprised!

What if you could work 24 hours a week, 7 months a year, and use the rest of your time to do whatever was important to you? Would you be willing to give it a try?

To start, you'll have to radically change the way that you approach your business or job. You'll need to deconstruct your pre-conceived platitudes of what success means on the deepest levels. Would you be a willing participant in this process if you knew there was a pot of gold waiting for you at the end of the virtual rainbow?

Then let's figure out a way to get your work done in those 24 hours for 28 weeks, make the money you need to support the perfect lifestyle you've created for yourself, and take five months a year off to pursue your passions and dreams!

It's your very own customized **24/7 Lifestyle Personal-Business Blueprint**.

It'll take a tremendous amount of self-discipline, time management, and dedication to accomplish this dream, but it can be done. If it's important, you will find the time, I guarantee it!

Stop coming up with excuses for why this isn't possible. There's never a perfect time to start an exercise routine, a diet, a new positive habit, or a new business. Obstacles will stand in your way and will play mind games with your brain, to convince you it can't be done or that you shouldn't do it.

There's always that nay-sayer voice inside your head asking, "What if you fail? What if you embarrass yourself?"

There are plenty of people in this struggling world who have it much worse than you. Just keep your problems in perspective. No matter how bad your day is, someone is having one that is much worse.

Make the 24/7 Lifestyle your guiding beacon and it'll help guide you when making all kinds of decisions. There are zillions of tips and tricks to help organize your time more efficiently. The more efficient you are with tasks, the more time you'll free up to do other things.

Here's a pretty simple way of looking at time management. In my opinion, you can't really manage time, but you can manage what you do with it. If you think like a "Next-Gen" time manager, it's more about what you don't do rather than what you do.

We're always learning about new and improved systems that allow us to accomplish more things in less time, thus freeing up more time to do other things. That's one of the great things about all the new technology! It allows us to do things more efficiently and stay focused on things that actually move the needle.

The way I organize my time each day is with what I call my POD system. Every activity is entered into a category, assigned a block of time, and placed on my schedule.

One trick that I always do is at the end of each week is sit down and plan the following week. I have some things that are in my schedule book for weeks and months in advance, but the day-to-day tasks that are necessary to keep the ship afloat are where the ultimate success lies.

On Monday morning, I have my game plan already in place and can be much more productive then simply allowing the wind to dictate where my time is spent.

For example, the first two hours of my day are always "Mitche" time. This includes listening to music or a podcast, reading the paper, reading a book, drinking a good cup of coffee, and setting my goals for the day.

This POD of time is circled in my schedule book. I don't allow anything to interrupt me during this time. I make sure I do not get distracted by email, texts from the previous day, social media timelines or notifications, and so on.

It's very important that this first POD of the day be completely controlled by you and you're not reacting to anything the world is dishing out.

In the Family POD, I get the kids fed, ready, and bussed off to school.

After that, the Reactive POD consists of replying to emails, returning phone calls, and anything else the world needs from me.

In the Revenue POD, I have a pre-defined list of objectives written down ahead of time.

After this Work POD, its back to either a personal or family POD to finish off the day. If you were to look at my schedule book, you would see a series of blocked out sections that are dedicated time slots for that activity. I'm not successful all the time, but I've developed a strong sense of purpose when it comes to sticking to my guns over the years.

This strategy is a good one if you assert your ability to keep outside influences from interrupting you. If you're in the middle of your personal POD, don't spend time on your phone looking at work emails or checking on online orders. If you're in your Revenue POD, don't allow yourself to be distracted with checking your Facebook timeline or looking up a recipe for tonight's dessert.

It's like putting out a virtual "DO NOT DISTURB" sign around your brain, then working like crazy to stay the course. Remember the nagging question: Does this activity or task help me attain my ultimate lifestyle goals?

If you begin your day in control of your time, you have a much better chance of ending the day that way. It's important that you do not give up your attention just because someone wants your face or phone time. The mistaken allure of social media has infested our social cultures faster than anything this world has ever seen. Regrettably, we're discovering more information every day about the side effects of spending too much time online, and how it is destroying our ability to focus on a task or have an attention span longer than that of a gnat!

At times, I feel like the "King of Remedial Jobs," which is a common skill set all entrepreneurs must have. You are the top-to-the-bottom, CEO of Toilets, The Answerer of Phones, The Runner of Errands, and of course the Shopper of Supplies.

All of it, everything falls into your lap when you are first starting out. We must do it all. To find out what you are good at and enjoy it, you must throw a massive amount of stuff on the wall to see what sticks.

The problem with having to do it all is that you end up doing everything half-assed. Your business was started because you had a passion for One-Thing, but you end up spreading that passion over a massive list of activities that are necessary to keep the car headed straight down the highway.

As a result, you become the Emperor of Mediocrity and nothing gets done correctly. This alone is the downfall of a majority of promising companies.

What is that One Thing you are absolutely the best at, and nobody can even hold a candle to you? What is the superpower that separates you from the rest of your competition and makes them shiver in their boots? If you can't answer that question immediately, you will need to grab a really good cup of coffee and spend some time with a pen and notebook!

I suck at many, many things, but I am world class at a couple of core competencies. Instead of whining about the things you suck at, you should be drilling down into the things are great at and hanging your hat on those.

If you are lucky enough to be good at what you like, develop a terminal case of tunnel vision! You may think that you have many talents, but there is something that you are so passionate about that it drives you daily to reach for the stars. Once you identify your single superpower, the rest of this journey becomes much easier.

If you can crack this code, that will be when you will experience explosive wealth and can ignite a clear vision of what path you must take.

Again, the most important question you can ask yourself is: Does this activity help me attain my ultimate lifestyle goals?

If it's not a hell yes, it needs to go into the hopper to determine its ultimate fate. You can ask these questions about every single activity or opportunity that comes up on a minute-by-minute basis.

The Golden Rule says 20% of our time and effort is spent on producing 80% of our positive results and output. Conversely, 80% of time is wasted on only 20% of our positive results and output. Knowing this, it will open up your way of thinking about every activity or task that your business makes. You can also use this hopper system to determine priorities in your personal life as well!

This is one of the most difficult decisions to make about the direction your business takes. Does this task or opportunity help you reach your business and personal goals? Is it necessary for you to incorporate this task into the fabric of your daily schedule? Can you cut some of the fat that automatically creeps into every business over time? Try not to hang onto it just because you may be emotionally attached or think that you must continue doing it. Remember, you want 20% of your efforts to result in 80% of your productive results.

STREAMLINE

Can you streamline the activity, so it takes the least amount of time to produce the maximum amount of results? Are there ways to automate the task and remove time-consuming activities? Time is the most valuable asset and resource you have on this earth. You need to ensure you're spending it on the most important things.

DELEGATE

Can you delegate the task to someone else? We have a very difficult time relinquishing power to anyone, especially if you're a small business owner where you are also Chief Bottle Washer-Custodian. Is there a way to train someone else to do the task 70% as proficient as you do it? Can you give them the tools and resources necessary to master the task more efficiently over time? You probably weren't an expert at the task when you first started, so keep that in mind when making this decision.

Can you delegate it to a virtual assistant, a contractor, or possibly hire a person specifically for this task? Giving up control invariably becomes a must if you plan on growing your business to a larger scale in the future. Remember that bigger isn't always better, especially when considering your definition of "the perfect life."

PROCRASTINATE

Is this a task that absolutely must be completed today, or can it be put off strategically into the future? Not because you are a lazy SOB who doesn't want to work, but rather it's something that is important, it just doesn't need to be accomplished today.

Let's take Bob's Lawn Service as an example of how to apply this principle. Bob is an entrepreneur who always dreamed of owning his own business. He quit his job and invested some money starting his professional lawn care company.

He purchased a new lawnmower, rakes, wheel barrels, gloves, and other paraphernalia needed to be successful with his new venture. Bob is the only employee and in charge of not only mowing all the lawns, but also marketing, networking, sales, website design, payables, and other tasks.

Bob managed to pick up several clients over a short time and eventually nearly filled up his schedule with recurring jobs every week. Not bad for a new business, but Bob knew how to work hard and smart.

One day, he received a call from the local shopping mall asking if he'd be interested in taking over the contract for their landscape maintenance. After meeting with management, Bob figured that he would need to spend nearly all his time during the week at the mall just to fulfill the contract.

That meant that all of his other clients would have to wait until after hours or weekends. The contract would exactly double his weekly revenue, so Bob had a hard time with the decision.

Let's put this opportunity into the hopper.

- Can Bob delegate the job to someone else? He could potentially hire a new employee to handle only the mall contract or handle the private residence contracts. That's certainly a possibility.

- Can he simply turn down the contract and eliminate the possibility altogether? Absolutely. But it depends on what Bob's ultimate goals are for growing his business.

- Can he streamline the task? Bob could purchase a larger lawnmower allowing him to finish his jobs much quicker, thus freeing up valuable time to handle more work. Great possibility!

- Can he procrastinate? Not if he wants the contract. He would not get the contract if he did not decide and then communicate with the client.

When Bob sat down to look at all his options, he remembered that his ultimate goal is to grow the business to the point where he can have employees handle all the lawn mowing, thus giving him more time to grow the business.

Most importantly, this strategy would give him more time to spend with his family.

Hence, Bob decided to bring on another employee and purchased a bigger lawnmower to handle the larger jobs. This freed up more time and allowed him to pick up five more commercial contracts.

Simply asking straight-forward questions can potentially revolutionize your business. Give yourself the creative freedom and passion to think out-of-the-box. You'll be amazed at what can transpire!

Recap:

- What is the one thing you are absolutely the best at, and nobody can even hold a candle to you?
- If you are lucky enough to be great at what you love, develop a terminal case of tunnel vision!
- You need to hang out with people who inspire you to think out-of-the-box.

Chapter 8
Traits of the Unleashed Entrepreneur

Now that you know about the unleashed life, let's discuss the qualities of truly passionate UEs. It's been said that if you love what you do for a living and are passionate about it, you won't have to work a day in your life. Many of us experience small moments of triumph throughout our lives. At those times, we love what we are doing and are passionate about it, even if only temporarily.

What about people who are passionate all the time? Do they know something we don't or is it something that can be developed and cultivated with time? There are several traits all passionate and successful people have in common.

Let's review some UE traits:

1. UEs have the right relationships, friendships, and networks. They hang around people who are enthusiastic and optimistic and stay away from people who bring them down. We all are a combination of the five people we spend the most amount of time with and we shouldn't waste time and energy on people who bring negativity into our world.

2. Get around big thinkers and thought leaders, or at least put yourself in an environment that is conducive to thinking big. UEs expose themselves to the newest and hottest trends and ideas. Educate yourself by reading a new magazine, trying new ideas out, listening to a business podcast, or watching an educational YouTube video!

3. New ideas and new intellectual input are essential to stoking the coals of our passion! Get yourself educated! Open your mind and look around you. See what other people are doing to acquire wealth and success, and then figure out creative ways to fold and adapt their ideas into your own.

4. I wake up early every day; that's when I get my best work done-no phones, no distractions, no emails, no people, no nothing... except for my brain and me. At night, my mind is mush, so mornings are when I do my planning, goal setting, and my best thinking. You need to identify what your "wheel house" time is for your best thinking.

5. UEs take advantage of opportunities that come their way. Opportunity is all over the place, but very few can see it because it usually involves change.

6. UEs are willing to take risks and make mistakes. The best teacher you will ever have is failure. It'll give you a whole new perspective on things. Just ask Mark Cuban, Richard Branson, and Elon Musk!

7. UEs are disciplined and tenacious. Tenacity is different from passion and commitment. It is perseverance that takes a task through to the end.

8. UEs are continuously educating themselves and applying what they learn. Many of us have read a book, watched a video, or went to a workshop that opened our minds to some new and creative technique, but you have to actually apply those ideas to your business and life.

A Secret about Education and Learning

Education and learning are like hearing a song on the radio. If you hear a song and you like it, you want to hear it again. If you hear it five times, you can sing along. If you hear it ten times, you can sing it on your own without the music. If you want to become a master at these techniques, ten times is the key.

The point, you ask? Good habits take time to create, and bad habits take time to break. Commit yourself to reading every important book you can get your hands on, watching every educational video, listening to every CD you come across, and going to seminars and workshops that focus on making you better!

Recap:

- If you love what you do, you won't have to work a day in your life.
- Hard work, perseverance, and dedication are the most important UE traits.

CHAPTER 9
Lighten Up!

A UE knows how to maintain a balanced life. Take your job seriously and yourself lightly. It's called having a sense of humor. If we can figure out a way to keep it light in the face of stress and change, we will be healthier, happier, and more fulfilled!

As you probably already know, stress is the number one killer in the United States. When things get difficult in our lives, we get overwhelmed with that feeling of uneasiness. Most stress is caused by change, but our world is overflowing with change every day!

Having a sense of humor is not something many are born with. This trait is a set of developed skills that allows us to be flexible in the face of stress and change, and it really has nothing to do with joke-telling even though most people associate it with that.

Do you feel you have a good sense of humor? There are humorless people in this wonderful world of ours going through life with a case of terminal professionalism. You know the type: "If I'm going to be successful, I must be hard driving, hard-headed. I must be serious. I don't have time to laugh and play around. Leave me alone. I'm having a really 'good' bad day!"

These people end up having nervous breakdowns, being our crotchety old neighbors, or dying prematurely from stress. We need to smile and get enjoyment from the simple things in life!

Humor won't solve many of the world's problems, but it sure makes it easier to get us through those tough days that pop up every now and then. It has the magical ability to sustain life.

When people are on their deathbeds, they don't say they wished they owned more toys or had more money. They say things like: "I wish I'd worked less and played more."

Benefits of Laughter

The effect of laughter on your body is immediate and amazing. When you laugh until your sides hurt, it can put a smile on your face that can last the entire day. Laughter can take the edge off a bad day and can enhance your good days even more.

After a good laugh, we have that feeling of being cleansed from head to toe. In fact, if it's a good laugh, the smile may last all day long!

Laughter triggers the release of endorphins, which is a pain killer produced by your brain. It's the same sensation that marathon runners feel from a euphoric high when they are running.

I don't know about you, but I would much rather spend time laughing every day instead of running a marathon to get that feeling of happiness!

I'm attracted to happy people because they put me in a better mood. Happiness is contagious. It spreads like the good flu. When one person is happy, the mood tends to spread to others!

Progress, Stress, and Change

Part of the reason we find it difficult to keep it light is that the world we live in is full of stress. Then again, stress isn't something that's new to mankind.

The guy who owned 1,000 horses people used for transportation heard about Henry Ford, but thought he had a great thing going and didn't pay close enough attention. He was eventually put out of business. The Walden Books and Barnes & Nobles of the world saw Amazon nipping at their heels, but kept their heads in the sand and slowly bled to death.

They didn't pay close attention and became nothing more than carcasses.

Netflix was but a little tickle in Blockbuster's side, but they had a vision for the future of entertainment. We know the ending to that sad story. In fact, Blockbuster could have bought Netflix way before they became a force in the industry. Nowadays, Netflix is a never-ending 24-hour streaming empire and a "force of nature" that dominates a large amount of our attention spans.

You either adapt or die. It's that simple. For those who think you can maintain your status quo, it just ain't gonna happen! You will end up as sludge like so many before you.

Keep your creative ideas fresh and continuously adjust your vision and objectives for your business. If you do, you will likely survive the future of radical changes that you will increasingly face.

Today, progress has vastly increased the accumulation of stressors, both actual and potential, in our lives. The Internet, smartphones, and other devices have become our conduit to the world, our entertainment centers, and are slowly replacing our relationships with family and friends.

No wonder we have such a difficult time keeping it light in the face of such radical changes. However, it's all a matter of perspective. Our thoughts can either keep us healthy or make us ill. It's all up to us. Being adaptable is one of the best traits you can cultivate.

Keeping Perspective

There is a wonderful place I like to go to in Mexico called Paamul. It's in the middle of nowhere with a bunch of bungalows, a restaurant, and a dive shop. That's it. It's the perfect place to get away from it all to recharge your batteries. The bungalows are only about 50 feet away from the Caribbean. If all my businesses weren't in the United States, I would probably spend at least six months a year down there. In my opinion, it's as close to heaven on earth as you can get. For those who need to stay connected, they even have wi-fi in the rooms.

My wife, Tami, on the other hand, looks at the accommodations with a different set of eyes. It's too far away from civilization, the bungalows are old and squeaky, you can smell the salt water mold and mildew at night when you sleep, and there are all sorts of little critters that fly around at night.

Over the years, Tami now admits she may be willing to spend a couple of months down there each year with our kids. Perhaps Pamuul is beginning to grow on her like the mold inside the bungalows.

The same reality produces different perspectives. What can be one person's heaven can be another person's nightmare! We are all hard-wired with a set of innate perspectives on how we view the world. Those wires are difficult to rewire, but they can be changed with the right tools and fuel.

Another way to keep your sense of humor is to remember that being successful has nothing to do with how much money you make or how many hours you work at the office. It's all about finding a proper balance in your life. We all need to be reminded from time to time that life is very short, fragile, and precious. I hope that you now have a new sense of what success means and are redefining your work/life balance.

Recap:

- Happiness is contagious. it spreads like the flu.
- Our thoughts can either keep us healthy or make us ill. it's up to us.
- Success is about finding a proper balance in your life.

CHAPTER 10
The Elephant in the Room

Can we talk?

First and foremost, I want to say I'm a firm believer in the power of social media (SM). If we're smart UEs, we use SM tools to our advantage. Today, business owners are facing an increasing demand on their time from a myriad of sources. The world has told us that we must become regular contributors to every SM platform or be left behind to rot.

The world must know what we're doing on a continuous basis or customers won't support our products and services, preferring to buy from others with more splashy SM banners and more active profiles. While it's true that SM has given us tons of possible tools to help grow revenue, it is by no means necessary to build a successful brand or business.

I'm addicted to knowledge. The Internet gives me access to everything I could ever want to know and then some about any topic I can imagine. Articles, videos, blogs, online courses, webinars, educational websites, and a never-ending smorgasbord of products and services are made to enrich our lives in one form or another.

What an amazing global marketplace for the UE to explore. My kids can learn about the history of Pompeii, how to build a Pinewood Derby car, or find out about the Monarch butterfly with the touch of their fingertips.

But there is something happening right before our very eyes. By the time we realize it, our businesses may be in real jeopardy of failure.

Listen. Do you hear that? It's the sound of your time being sucked right out from underneath you. You have voluntarily traded your attention span and time for a small amount of gratification that may or may not have anything to do with your ultimate goals. You have freely given of our most precious resource, your time, in exchange for an adrenaline rush for a millisecond, when your face is buried in our device.

On average, we check our emails 150 times a day, and there are 2 billion people that spend 50 minutes a day on Facebook and Instagram. That doesn't even include time spent watching YouTube videos of stupid cat tricks, creating silly videos on Snapchat, or tweeting a picture of what you ate for dinner.

Using SM provides us with immediate rewards for very little effort, and your brain begins to desire more stimulation.

It's a vicious circle of doom. For me, I prefer to utilize my limited bandwidth for more productive activities.

You can create the perfect lifestyle for you and your family and build the most fantastic business in the world, only to have it all fall apart because you don't have the self-discipline to say no to the call of the Internet siren. Just because somebody or something asks for your time doesn't mean you need to give it up so easily!

All SM platforms were created with a single mission: to make money! They have done this by creating communities of fans and selling that attention to sponsors for cash. They deliver value to us, the customer, and that value has a price tag on it in the form of various ads.

I admit that trying to control your online habits is a bit like fighting a Hydra, but you need to control your urges if you want to realize your maximum potential.

Many of you may be yelling at me right now. That's okay. I can take it.

With that said, I only want the best for every single business person who has a dream and is willing to risk making those dreams come true.

There are many other resources out there that teach you how to utilize the Internet in appropriate ways, but here are some tips and tricks that may help you resist the urge to stay up until midnight browsing Facebook.

1. Give yourself an hour in the morning before looking at your device or logging on to your computer. Your device will be waiting for you, I promise.

2. Create device-free zones in your house. You can talk to your spouse and children without them checking their text messages every 45 seconds.

3. Set up a block of time (POD) during your day when you can respond to these demands on your time. If you set aside some time for the Internet, it will prevent you from being side-tracked during the time you're focused on other projects.

The bottom line is this. To build the lifestyle of your dreams in productive alignment with the business of your dreams, you will need to master your control over the use of the Internet. It's that simple.

I believe we all have become victims, but it's not too late to take back control of our time and reinvest it into creating your perfect lifestyle!

Recap:

- Listen. Do you hear that? It's the sound of your time being sucked out from underneath you.

- Responding to every text, email, or notification is like having a mini slot machine attached to your hand. It's highly addictive and can destroy a dream.

- Just because somebody asks you for your time doesn't mean you have to give it to them.

- Being able to control your urges is a vital skill set if you want to achieve your maximum potential.

CHAPTER 11
Popcorn With Mitche

Designing your perfect life can be one of the most enjoyable experiences you can ever explore. It allows you to get to know yourself on an intimate level and can give your business a world-class jolt of adrenaline. It will not be easy by any stretch of your imagination, but that's why very few people are entrepreneurs.

I believe our ability to ask and work through difficult questions about how we view the world is an absolute must if we want to reap the benefits of thinking like a true UE.

First, envision the vision and set your goals. Painting the masterpiece that is your life needs a healthy dose of creative thinking, followed by reverse-engineering your business and setting goals to help you achieve that vision. There is no quick fix that will give you the success you dream of, but there are simple questions you can ask yourself to shake the bushes and keep the cobwebs from creeping into your brain.

As we have discussed in detail, designing your perfect lifestyle is a matter of perspective and philosophy. It's much more than the car you drive, the house you live in, or the amount of money in your 401k.

It's about gaining control over your precious time, so you can enjoy each special moment that comes your way without distractions.

It takes a very special person to keep their nose to the grindstone each and every day. My goal for you is that you'll begin to replace negative habits in your life with positive, productive habits that will ignite your dreams like never before. If you are a business owner, you know the joy of doing inventory at the end of each month.

I call this the Popcorn Exercise. At the end of the process, you will have a firm grasp on everything that is inside of your Life Warehouse. The more information you have about yourself, the better equipped you will be to create the kind of life that you have always wanted.

We need to be acutely aware of who we are and what motivates us. That is why spending time with yourself is an important part of your daily routine. Grab a pen, a notepad, a good cup of coffee, and hit your back deck for a while.

You are going to break your life down into three categories: Personal, Family, and Professional. This exercise intends to get your life, as it exists today, onto a piece of paper:

PERSONAL

- Do you get upset at yourself for not sticking to your diet and exercise program? Describe what your current diet and exercise routines are, then write a new plan with new routines you will begin.

- Are you satisfied with your spiritual growth? Do you attend church services as much as you would like? If you are not religious, do you spend adequate time in personal or alone time so you're in touch with your internal voice? Write out a plan for your personal development.

- What hobbies are you involved in? Do you spend as much time as you would like participating in them? Write out a plan for what activities you would like to pursue.

- Have you given up some of your passions because of children or career? Would you want to make them part of your life again?

- What do you like about yourself? Can you improve on those things?
- What don't you like about yourself? Can you improve on those things?

The purpose of the Popcorn Exercise is to "rattle your brain" a little and remove the cobwebs. Once you have brainstormed about your life as it exists today, it's time to give some thought about where you want your life to be tomorrow and begin building your perfect lifestyle.

Brainstorm for a Breakthrough

You have already hand-crafted your perfect lifestyle, so now it's time to set goals in order to make that happen. Grab a stack of 3x5 index cards and let the creative juices flow! You are going to write down your personal and professional goals for the next 12 months. Your personal goals should be done before the others. You started this process earlier, so it should be easy to add to your chicken scratches and notes.

Do you want to take a vacation this year? Do you have your eye on a special boat or set of golf clubs? How about your garden? Would you like to spend more time cultivating it or working in the yard?

What about other hobbies you haven't had time for recently? If it's important to you, then you should make the time in your schedule to read, write, paint, or play with the family dog.

Write down one goal per note card. What projects have you been meaning to start or finish? Where do you want to be in one month, three months, a year, or five years? What new hobbies do you want to learn? What old hobbies and interests would you like to bring back into your life? What projects have you been putting off because you just didn't have the time? Where do you want to go on vacation? What about your family? Would you like to spend more quality time with each of them individually? Write it all down on a note card. This is the next step towards designing your perfect lifestyle.

You may have an entire stack of things you've been meaning to get to, but have not dedicated the necessary time.

This exercise must be done at a time and place where you won't be interrupted or distracted. From spending just 15 minutes a day immersed in setting goals for your life and brainstorming, you will begin to create positive habits that will stick with you for the rest of your life. Once you come up with an idea, write it down. After you put it on paper, it will be much easier to expand the idea and develop it into creative breakthroughs.

Prioritize (The Salsa Box)

Now it's time to prioritize and organize your goals. If you tried to complete everything in your stack, I venture to say you would fail miserably and get disgusted with yourself in the process. Instead of eating the whole pizza all at once, you need to eat one slice at a time, so set some realistic goals.

Categorize your goals into three groups, similar to Level I, Level II, and Level III "perfect days" that I described in Chapter 6. Goals or projects that you can't wait to get started on can be placed into the "hot" section of your salsa box. Items that are a little more long-term can be put into the "medium" category. Lastly, things that are long term, or possibly things you may never get to, can be put into the "mild" section.

Your "Salsa Goal Box" will make it easier to establish some realistic time lines for your goals. By having everything already written down in your Salsa Goal Box, you will increase your chances of success.

Share

If you want this to truly make a difference in your life, you must become accountable to at least one other living person. It may be your spouse, your business partner, or your best friend, but it should be someone who understands and supports you. Set a time where you can lay out your game plan and share your goals and aspirations with them.

Ask the other person to make sure to hold your feet to the fire on occasion so you don't get lazy. If you set up a weekly conversation with them to discuss how things are going, you will allow the other person to be involved with your efforts in a very personal way.

Take Action

Once you have established your list of goals and shared them with a confidant, it's time to put your money where your mouth is. Putting some of your goals into motion can be a revolutionary step! Don't make up excuses or come up with reasons why you can't do something. Just go and get it done.

As you put this program into action and begin to emulate passionate successful people, choose something small that you will be able to accomplish easily and dedicate yourself to doing it every day for one week.

Maybe it's something as simple as going for a short walk at lunch, spending 30 minutes every day reading self-improvement books, working on sales projections for next quarter, going through boxes in your basement, or maybe stopping on the way home to visit a friend who's been feeling down lately.

Once you begin to make these small items part of your daily routine, the bigger things won't seem quite so daunting and overwhelming. The smallest things can make the biggest difference.

Recap:

- Do not sell your precious time to the highest bidder.
- Passionate people are developed.
- If you want to truly make a difference in your life, you must be accountable to at least one other living person.

CHAPTER 12
How Are You Spending Your Dash?

Can you tell me what the following numbers are?

1825-1877

1776-1851

1962- 2003

They are life spans. There's a born-on date and a dead-on date. We have little control over either one of those events, but what we do have control over is what we do with the time in-between. It's called the "dash." It's everything that happens from the second you were born to the moment you die. It's your entire life boiled down into a minuscule hyphen!

The question I'd like you to marinate in your mind is: How are you spending your dash?

The dash is all you have to leave behind when you are done with your time on Earth. Are you making a difference in the lives of people who mean the most to you?

Now that you are done reading this book, I hope you have gained a renewed perspective on what's important in your life. Living the life of a UE means much more than running a successful business, it means living a life of meaning and purpose as well.

Another way of describing the in-between segment of your life is the gap. Here's where you are, there's where you want to be, and then there's the gap in between. We need to learn to love the gap because that's where most of our life is lived. Gap Thinking will help you understand the importance of your dash.

We all want to be better dads, moms, friends, bosses, and workers. We want to live a life that is rewarding and fulfilling, yet success and happiness seems to elude many people. A large number of people are mired in jobs they hate, marriages that are broken, and other quagmires. We all need something to strive for, work towards, and dream about.

What's your reason for getting out of bed every day? If you can't come up with a better reason than "I have to," then it's time to take a hard look at your life from 40,000 feet.

If you were to ask a group of elderly people what they would do differently if they could live their life all over again, I venture to say that 95 percent would answer that they would reflect more, risk more, and do more things that would live on after they were gone. The best part is that we don't have to wait until our life is nearly over before we can begin to live like this. You can begin today.

There's nothing sadder to me than when someone doesn't give their life enough value, or when someone says:

"I didn't live my life like I should have. I didn't achieve, I didn't take any risks."

There's no going back to the beginning of the race.

When you go to sleep every night, it's one less day you have. Can you imagine getting up, going to work, and having to do things you don't like to do or are not very good at? That's not the kind of thing that makes you get up every day with a spring in your step.

But when you get up with a sense of purpose and you love what you do, it's going to bring your focus into a very narrow beam of high-intensity energy bursting with very palpable results.

What's holding you back from living the life of your dreams? What steps can you take today to make those dreams come true? I've noticed many people do not have a real sense of direction, almost as if they were waiting for someone to show them the way. You must make the choice to move forward with your life and not sit around waiting for the magic to happen from out of the blue.

There are two kinds of people in this world: Those who wait for something to happen, and those who take the initiative and make things happen. If you need to change, don't make any more excuses.

Hoping that things will change has no effect. Only tangible actions on your part will make the difference!

Life is a very delicate balance. The challenge is to keep your perspective and discover or rediscover what's important to you. We never know when our time is up. Most people live like they are bubble gum wrappers in a parking lot, meandering wherever the wind blows them to.

Today matters, so use what you have to make someone else's life better!

Living Like You Mean It

If you want to make the most of your life and live it with enthusiasm and zeal, reading this book will not be enough. You will need to make some tough decisions along the way. Your approach to life will need to change. As your approach changes, your attitude and the way you allocate your time will as well.

Any type of transformation requires a process of accepting change. We are constantly in "process" of becoming whatever we are meant to be. With the right attitude, EVERY DAY IS A SATURDAY!

Will you start that transformation today?

A SPECIAL THANK YOU NOTE

I truly appreciate you taking the time to invest in your quality of life, your business, and your future! If you found the book to be beneficial, I would be grateful if you would leave a 5-Star review on Amazon. It would mean the world to me!

To sign up for a FREE membership in our *Unleashed Tribe* Newsletter, I invite you to visit our website at www.PowerMarketing101.com. Enter the code **"UETRIBE"** to receive a complimentary bonus.

Looking for more inspiration and actionable tools to grow your business and design your perfect lifestyle? Then subscribe to the hottest new show ***The Unleashed Entrepreneur Podcast*** on iTunes or Stitcher. Hear dynamic interviews with world-class Entrepreneurs as well as regular dose of meat-and-potatoes techniques that will ignite your superpower to achieve even greater things!

Thank you for spending this time with me, and good luck with your new set of eyes!

Mitche

www.ingramcontent.com/pod-product-compliance
Lightning Source LLC
Chambersburg PA
CBHW060042210326
41520CB00009B/1236